HOW THE FUTURE BEGAN:

EVERYDAY LIFE

HOW THE FUTURE BEGAN:

EVERYDAY LIFE

CLIVE GIFFORD

KINGFISHER

NEW YORK

Author
Clive Gifford

Senior Editor
Clive Wilson

Designer
Veneta Altham

DTP Co-ordinator
Nicky Studdart

Production Controller
Jacquie Horner

Picture Research Manager
Jane Lambert

Picture Researcher
Juliet Duff

Indexer
Hilary Bird

KINGFISHER
Larousse Kingfisher Chambers Inc.
95 Madison Avenue
New York, New York 10016

First published in 2000
1 3 5 7 9 10 8 6 4 2
1TR/0300/TWP/RNB/135NYMA

LIBRARY OF CONGRESS CATALOGING–IN–PUBLICATION DATA
has been applied for.

ISBN 0-7534-5268-5
Printed in Singapore

CONTENTS

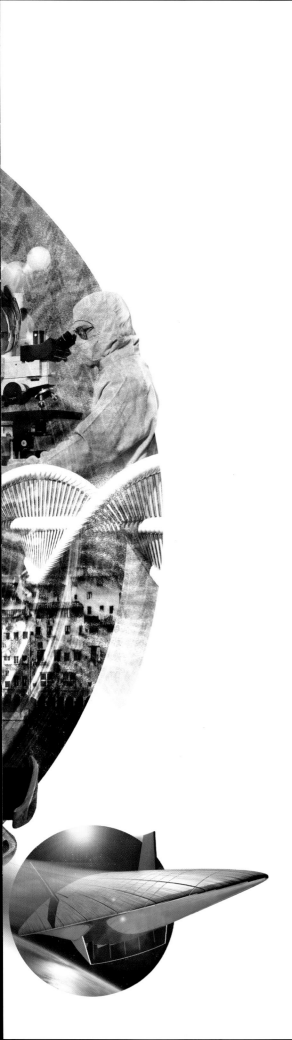

INTRODUCTION

During the 21st century, we will witness great changes in our everyday lives. Breakthroughs in fields as diverse as medicine, communications, architecture, and transportation will have a major impact on society. Most people will live in cities, which will continue to grow outward as well as upward. Inside your intelligent home, sensors will detect your presence and automatically adjust the environment. If you own a car, it will probably be a non-polluting, electric model. For longer journeys, new forms of propulsion will cut the journey times for train, sea, and air travel.

New technologies will continue to power the Information Revolution. The next generation of virtual reality and holographic communication systems will have far-reaching effects on areas such as education and the way we work. Advances in health care and medicine will lead to a significant increase in life expectancy and, one day, gene therapy may even be able to prevent most diseases.

Everyday life for people in developed countries will be safer and more productive than ever before. However, many important issues will still need to be addressed. These will include serious water and food shortages in many parts of the world; overcrowding in cities; pollution; and the consequences of an increasingly aging population. Biotechnology and genetic engineering will benefit millions of people, but concerns about the potential misuse of these new technologies are also likely to continue.

1999
Petronas Towers, world's tallest building, completed in Malaysia

1970s
Use of composite materials

1934
Fluorescent light invented

1931
Empire State Building completed

1892
Reinforced concrete invented

1885
First skyscraper built in Chicago

1779
Completion of first all-metal bridge in England

3500 B.C.
First cities appear in Mesopotamia (now Iraq)

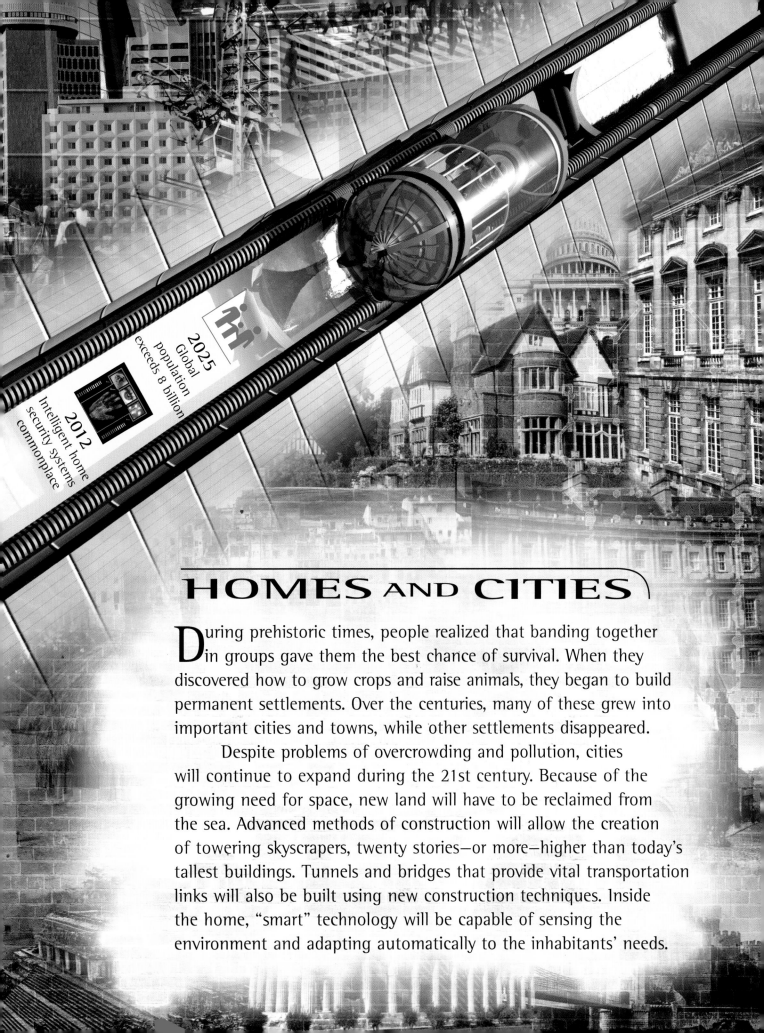

2025
Global population exceeds 8 billion

2012
Intelligent home security systems commonplace

HOMES AND CITIES

During prehistoric times, people realized that banding together in groups gave them the best chance of survival. When they discovered how to grow crops and raise animals, they began to build permanent settlements. Over the centuries, many of these grew into important cities and towns, while other settlements disappeared.

Despite problems of overcrowding and pollution, cities will continue to expand during the 21st century. Because of the growing need for space, new land will have to be reclaimed from the sea. Advanced methods of construction will allow the creation of towering skyscrapers, twenty stories—or more—higher than today's tallest buildings. Tunnels and bridges that provide vital transportation links will also be built using new construction techniques. Inside the home, "smart" technology will be capable of sensing the environment and adapting automatically to the inhabitants' needs.

FUTURE CITY

Since the development of the first large settlements over 5,000 years ago, people have been living and working in cities and towns. Two hundred years ago, only two and half percent of the world's population lived in urban areas. By 2005, over half of the world's population will live in cities, and this figure is expected to keep growing until at least the mid-21st century. The attraction of the city as a seat of power, work, learning, and recreation will continue despite the potential problems created by overcrowding, pollution, and the demands of a growing population.

△ Athens, the capital of Greece, was the most powerful city in the world 2,500 years ago. Its public buildings have inspired architects and builders ever since.

△ Some cities evolve over many centuries. Others, such as Los Angeles, have expanded over a shorter period. In 1890, Los Angeles had a population of 50,000. Today, over nine million people live there.

△ As cities grow, they tend to spread out, as shown in this satellite picture of London, England. Towns and villages, once outside the city, are swallowed up and become part of the urban sprawl.

Stealing space

Space for living, working, transportation, and recreation is limited in cities and will remain a key urban issue in the future. In the 1900s, cities grew skyward, as well as continuing to sprawl out into the countryside. In the future, it is likely that city planners will create space underground for living and working.

Out at sea

Projects to reclaim land from swamps, marshes, and oceans will flourish in wealthy, but small, nations as a way of increasing available space. There is also the possibility of separate, floating cities, or hybrid, part-floating, part-landbound settlements, linked to the mainland. One proposed scheme is designed to provide living and working space for a million people in a huge, pyramid-shaped structure on the sea off Tokyo, Japan.

▽ As future cities expand, they will make use of all available space, including water, if possible. Environmentally-friendly forms of transportation, like airships, will ferry people around this 2030 metropolis.

◁ Air pollution is a major problem that many cities face. Smog created by factories, power plants, and automobile traffic can cause health problems.

Cyber city

Cyberjaya, a city being built in Malaysia, may provide a model for 21st-century cities. In Cyberjaya, gas-fueled vehicles will be banned, low population density—less crowded living—will be encouraged, and every home will be powered by solar energy and connected to the City Command Center—a computer network that provides automated services.

◁ During the English Industrial Revolution in the 1700s and 1800s, many people lived in run-down housing, or slums, when they moved from the countryside to the city.

LIVING TOGETHER

With huge improvements in health care and breakthroughs in the fight against disease, the population of planet earth is booming. It is estimated that by 2025 there will be eight billion people; the number could rise to nine billion in only ten more years. This fast-growing population will place an enormous strain on cities, many of which already suffer from overcrowding and other associated problems. Concerns about traffic control, pollution, and the psychological problems resulting from people living very close together will continue into the 21st century.

Social problems

Crowding people together in housing units or skyscrapers is not the best solution to the problem of finding homes for people. In the past, this kind of high-density living has led to major social problems such as drug abuse and violent crime. The search for more humane ways of housing greater numbers of people will become an important issue in many future cities.

▷ Not all traffic jams are caused by cars. Bicycle rickshaws have created this gridlock in Dhaka, Bangladesh. Unlike cars, however, they are nonpolluting.

This capsule hotel in Tokyo makes maximum use of the limited living space in the city. Hotel guests sleep in tiny units that are stacked on top of each other.

Designs for living

In existing cities, run-down areas will be redeveloped to house the growing population. In some cases, high-density living and working space will be crammed into a small area. Mass transit systems and moving walkways will ferry people around. Other areas may choose a low-density, community-led approach with smaller buildings, parks, and car-free zones.

▷ Hong Kong, China, is one of the world's most crowded places. With limited affordable housing, slums are usually the only alternative.

◁ Enclosed walkways at different levels will form an extensive network connecting many parts of the city. People will be able to move around without having to negotiate the congested streets.

Getting away from it all

From 2010, it is likely that an increasing number of people will turn their backs on city living. Many will move to small cities and towns to escape pollution, congestion, and other urban problems. Advanced communications technology will enable them to telecommute—work from home. Others may go further and opt out of the "rat race" altogether, living in self-sustaining communities in isolated areas.

BLURRED VISION

This imaginary flying city from a 1920s science fiction magazine is one unlikely solution to overcrowding on the planet. Writers and artists have imagined airborne cities since the 1700s.

FUTURE HOMES

In the future, new houses will be designed to cocoon their inhabitants in a secure, comfortable, and highly adaptable environment. Architects, engineers, and designers will draw on important advances in material technology and electronics to create flexible living spaces that can be altered easily by the occupants. Intelligent devices will play an important role in many households. Robot cleaners and smart exercise machines that monitor people's health will be as common as today's microwave ovens and washing machines.

△ Before the 1800s, few homes had any luxuries or comforts. Until labor-saving devices like vacuum cleaners and washing machines appeared in the 1900s, all housework had to be done by hand and it usually took a long time.

◁ Architects and engineers are rethinking how a house functions both inside and out. This house in California is earthquake resistant and incorporates the latest in energy-saving technology.

Intelligent home

Experts predict that by 2025 the average home will have as much computing power as a nuclear power plant from the 1990s. Computers will be so small and cheap that they will be embedded, or integrated, in almost all our surroundings, from floors to fridges. They will sense our presence and automatically adjust the environment—including light, temperature, and humidity levels—according to our needs.

Flexible living

Formal divisions between rooms are likely to disappear. They will be replaced by a single living space that can be sectioned off with lightweight, but soundproof, movable walls. Multipurpose furniture will occupy living areas. Furniture structure and coverings will change color, shape, and even texture at the user's request. New materials will allow a soft bench seat to transform itself into a table or desk, for example.

▽ The home of 2015 will include furniture that can change its shape and color, and walls that serve as giant display screens for information, recreation, or simply to create a relaxing environment. A robot vacuum cleaner will automatically detect and clean up spills.

▷ Alternative forms of energy such as wind and solar power will provide all the energy requirements for an increasing number of homes in the future.

▽ Keys will be replaced by biometric systems that scan a person's features before allowing access (*below right*).

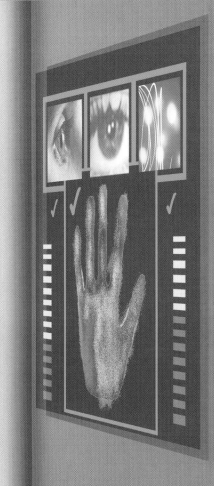

Safe and secure

Traditional locks and keys will be replaced by security systems that scan a person's hand, eye, or face and use biometrics to determine who can enter. Arrays of closed-circuit TV (CCTV) cameras will be linked to a network of home security sensors far more sophisticated than today's burglar alarms. If an unauthorized person tries to enter, the house will lock up like a clam and automatically notify the police. It may even use gas sprays or hoses that "fire" harmless sticky foam to prevent the intruder from escaping.

△ Some architects and builders are rejecting the latest technology in favor of simple homes constructed from natural, locally-sourced materials.

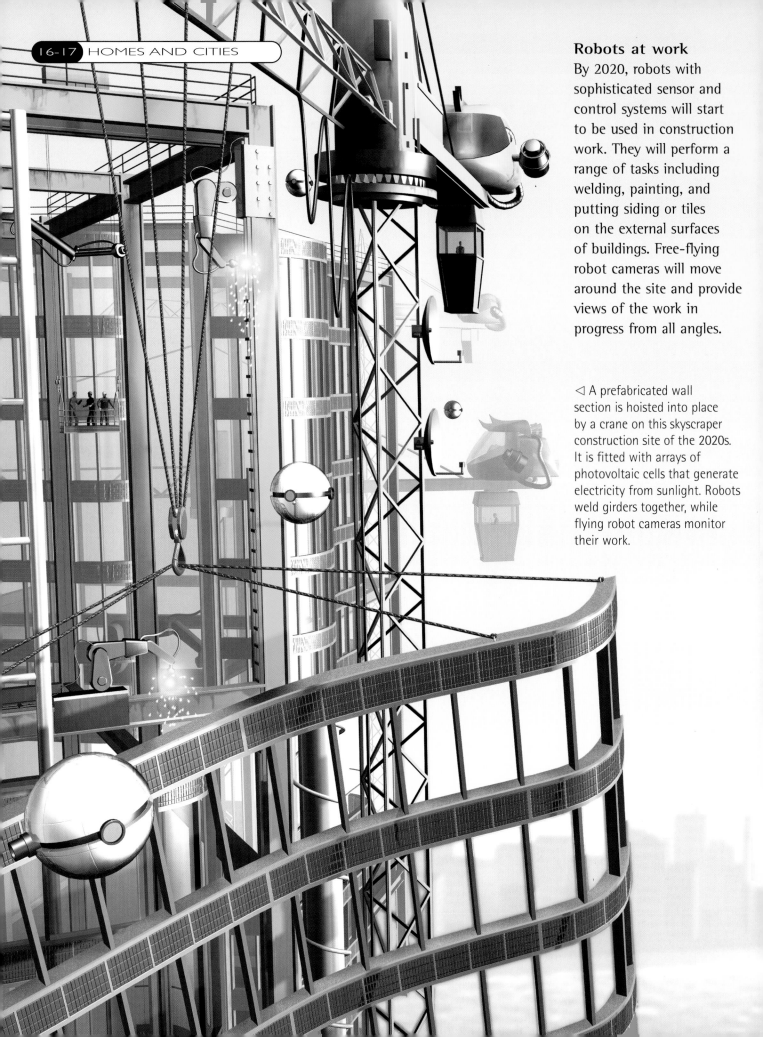

Robots at work

By 2020, robots with sophisticated sensor and control systems will start to be used in construction work. They will perform a range of tasks including welding, painting, and putting siding or tiles on the external surfaces of buildings. Free-flying robot cameras will move around the site and provide views of the work in progress from all angles.

◁ A prefabricated wall section is hoisted into place by a crane on this skyscraper construction site of the 2020s. It is fitted with arrays of photovoltaic cells that generate electricity from sunlight. Robots weld girders together, while flying robot cameras monitor their work.

◁ Construction of the Empire State Building began in March 1930 and was completed in May 1931. It has 102 stories and contains over 178 miles (285km) of steel beams.

Hazard proof
Earthquakes pose a serious threat to some of the world's major cities including San Francisco and Tokyo, Japan. New construction techniques are helping to make some structures more earthquake resistant. The Tokyo Forum building, for example, has glass walls supported independently of the roof. During an earthquake, the roof rocks on powerful joints, preventing the building from crashing down.

CONSTRUCTION

Materials are at the very heart of the construction industry. In the foreseeable future, buildings will continue to be built using steel, concrete, bricks, and glass, but composite materials and metal alloys will also be used. These new materials, along with advanced computer modeling, will allow architects and engineers to design even bigger buildings, tunnels, and bridges and to construct them in places that are currently considered unsuitable. A further innovation will be tiny sensors inside the materials that automatically measure and report any deterioration.

△ Geodesic domes are strong, lightweight structures that do not require internal supports. They are able to enclose large areas using less material than standard frames.

Bridging the gap
Some of the most important construction projects are bridges. The development of exceptionally strong materials, along with computer modeling, is allowing engineers to design increasingly ambitious structures. Proposed projects include the 2 mile (3.3km) long Messina Straits Bridge to link mainland Italy and Sicily, and a 3 mile (5km) long bridge across the Straits of Gibraltar to join Europe and North Africa.

▷ The 1,506 ft. (451m) high Petronas Towers in Malaysia have over 32,000 windows.

◁ Powerful computers allow engineers to test structures for stresses and strains long before they are built.

CRYSTAL BALL

An increasing number of homes will be built underground during the 21st century. Underground homes offer a spacious alternative to cramped conditions on the surface, and are naturally cool, even in very hot climates.

TRANSPORTATION

Until the middle of the 1800s, most people rarely traveled more than a few miles from their homes. When they set out on a journey, their travel choices were limited—boat, ship, horse, or foot. With the invention of the steam locomotive in the 1800s, and later the development of road vehicles and aircraft, modern transportation opened up a whole new world for many people. During the 21st century, many forms of transportation will become faster, safer, and less harmful to the environment. Electric-powered cars, which cause minimal pollution, will be commonplace on the roads by 2025. Shipping and rail will also benefit from exciting new forms of power such as magnetic propulsion. For longer journeys, hypersonic and suborbital airliners could cut flying time by up to two thirds.

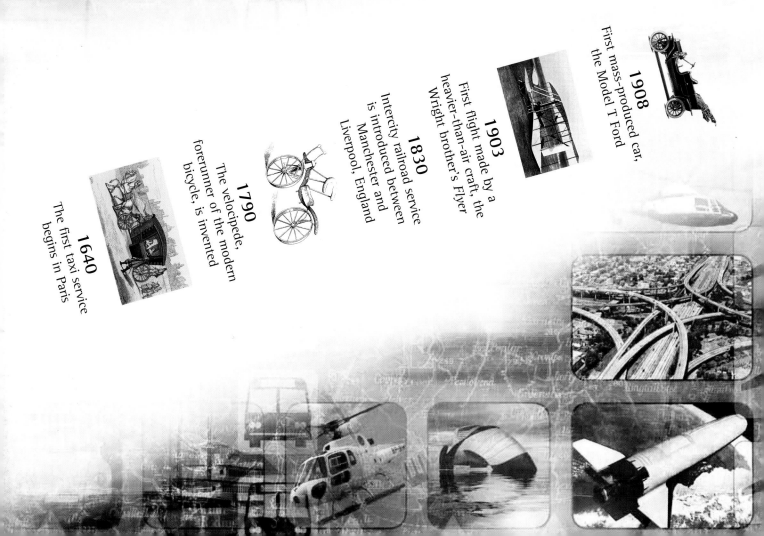

1640
The first taxi service begins in Paris

1790
The velocipede, forerunner of the modern bicycle, is invented

1830
Intercity railroad service is introduced between Manchester and Liverpool, England

1903
First flight made by a heavier-than-air craft, the Wright brother's Flyer

1908
First mass-produced car, the Model T Ford

1959
First commercial hovercraft
service in operation

1981
French TGV high-speed
train service introduced

2010
New generation of safe
airships carries passengers
and heavy goods

2035
It takes under two hours to
fly halfway across the world

▽ Concept 2096 is one research team's vision of the car for the end of the century. Passengers will be encased in an extremely tough protective shell. The car will be driven automatically using guide transmitters located on streets and roads.

△ Early cars looked like horseless carriages. The Lutzmann car, built in 1895, was powered by a simple internal combustion engine.

FUTURE CAR

When the first cars took to the roads in the 1880s and 1890s, their top speed rarely exceeded 12 mph. (20km/h). The brakes were usually ineffective and engines often exploded. A century ago, no one could have predicted the global increase in road vehicles, which today number hundreds of millions. Modern cars may be faster, more comfortable, and more fuel-efficient than their predecessors, but, like the first cars, they rely mostly on pollution-causing oil derivatives. The future is likely to see popular alternatives to purely gasoline-powered vehicles—machines that offer comparable performance but at a lower cost to the planet.

△ Most of today's electric cars have a limited range and can only travel about 60 miles (100km) before their batteries need to be recharged. This recharging point is built into a parking space in Los Angeles.

Fighting pollution

Although modern internal combustion engine cars are "cleaner" than in the past, their exhaust emissions still cause damage to the atmosphere. Many suggestions have been made about how to lessen the impact. These include more fuel-efficient and lightweight cars and an increase in electric vehicle production. Other initiatives include the promotion of public transportation and the banning of cars from urban centers.

△ The Ford *Synergy* is a prototype vehicle driven by hybrid propulsion. It could be in production by 2010.

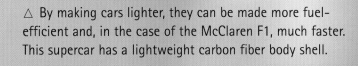

△ By making cars lighter, they can be made more fuel-efficient and, in the case of the McClaren F1, much faster. This supercar has a lightweight carbon fiber body shell.

A host of extras

Despite joystick-controlled prototypes, the steering wheel is likely to remain a part of cars in the future. However, steering and other driver tasks such as navigation, braking, and gear changing will benefit from advances in onboard computer systems. Drivers will also use voice-activated mapping and route trackers, and their e-mail will be read to them using a speech synthesizer.

Best of both worlds

Hybrid propulsion offers a compromise between clean, electric-powered cars and high-performance, gasoline models. The electric motor, which gives off no emissions, is operated in built-up areas and at low speeds. On the open road, away from urban areas, the gasoline engine takes over. Hybrid cars cause up to ten times less pollution than conventional cars and are expected to be a popular type of vehicle by 2010.

BLURRED VISION

Predictions that self-driving vehicles would take to the roads by 2000 were wide of the mark. However, in the near future, powerful sensors and more effective control systems will help drivers and make road trips safer.

ON THE ROAD

△ During the 1900s, many cities suffered from serious road congestion. This scene from 1912 shows a traffic jam in the center of London.

By 2015, a growing number of cities and towns will encourage the use of bikes, electric-powered, single person vehicles, and new mass transit initiatives. However, the most extensive change to road transportation will be Intelligent Traffic Systems (ITS). By 2020, ITS may be in use in the U.S., Japan, and Europe. ITS use computer networks to manage traffic, keep vehicles a set distance apart, and advise drivers on the best routes. Its advocates promise less congested roads, a reduction in accidents, and huge savings in fuel consumption because of more efficient route planning.

Traffic management

Advanced Intelligent Traffic Systems will be based on a sophisticated network of sensors. These will map an entire road journey and communicate with computers in the car. By 2025, cars may travel in a convoy, each car's speed and distance from other vehicles being controlled automatically in a system called platooning.

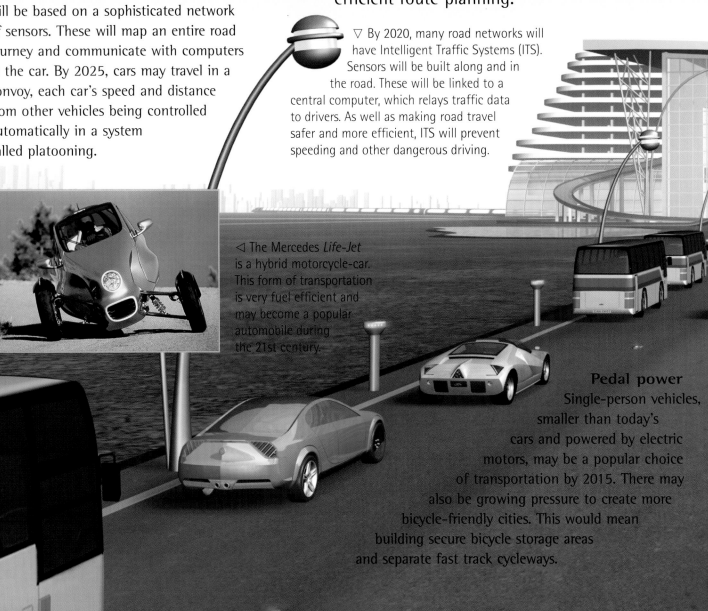

▽ By 2020, many road networks will have Intelligent Traffic Systems (ITS). Sensors will be built along and in the road. These will be linked to a central computer, which relays traffic data to drivers. As well as making road travel safer and more efficient, ITS will prevent speeding and other dangerous driving.

◁ The Mercedes *Life-Jet* is a hybrid motorcycle-car. This form of transportation is very fuel efficient and may become a popular automobile during the 21st century.

Pedal power

Single-person vehicles, smaller than today's cars and powered by electric motors, may be a popular choice of transportation by 2015. There may also be growing pressure to create more bicycle-friendly cities. This would mean building secure bicycle storage areas and separate fast track cycleways.

Self diagnosis

By 2010, many cars will be built with a fully integrated central computer connected to sensors throughout the car. The computer will monitor many aspects of performance: from brake quality to engine timing. The computer will automatically maximize performance and efficiency, warn of potential malfunctions, and communicate directly with a car repair company. Using a system called telemetry, the repair service may even be able to diagnose and fix certain internal faults by remote control.

△ The Urban Dream bicycle is a new type of folding bike that uses lightweight materials to make it easier to carry. These bikes are light enough to carry in one hand, and are ideal for commuters to move quickly around cities.

▷ The recumbent bicycle may be a common sight on roads in the future. Cycling in this position places less stress on the body, allowing the cyclist to travel faster for longer distances.

◁ Advanced electronic entertainment will be an optional feature in most automobiles by 2010. Special screens fitted to the seat backs will provide games, movies, and Internet access.

◁ Before the invention of the steam-powered locomotive in the 1800s, wagons and carts pulled by animals were the fastest methods of moving goods by land.

FERRYING PEOPLE AND GOODS

Civilizations—both past and present—have always depended on the effective transportation of supplies, materials, goods, and people. The invention of engine-powered vehicles, in the early 1800s, dramatically increased the speed of transportation and the amount of freight that could be moved. A growth in population means not only a greater demand for goods and materials, but also greater pressure on public transportation. It is estimated that by 2023, passengers across the world will travel more than 55 trillion miles (88 trillion km)—twice today's figure. Alternative modes of transportation, such as magnetic levitation trains and airships, are expected to ease some of the pressure.

△ Standardized containers have transformed the way cargo is moved around the world. Railcars, lifting apparatus, trucks, and ships form a fully integrated transportation system.

Airship revival

Airships were a popular form of transportation until a series of accidents in the 1920s and 1930s. Currently they use nonflammable gas and are expected to make a comeback, especially as freight carriers. Although airships are slow, they can carry heavy cargo. By 2020, 400-yard airships will be capable of carrying up to 300 tons of cargo over distances of more than 5,000 miles (8,000km).

△ The Transrapid monorail link is expected to open in Germany in 2005. It will connect the cities of Hamburg and Berlin, carrying passengers at speeds over 300 mph. (500km/h).

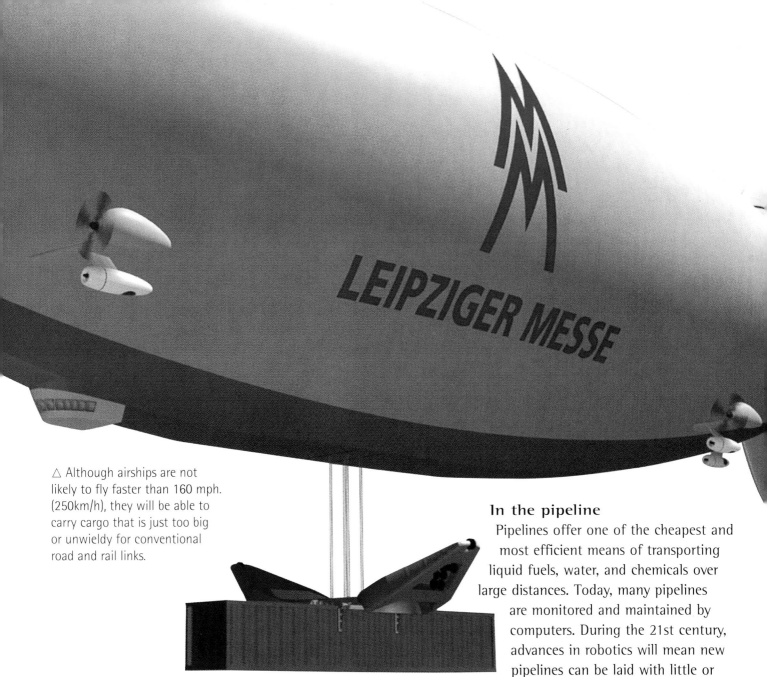

△ Although airships are not likely to fly faster than 160 mph. (250km/h), they will be able to carry cargo that is just too big or unwieldy for conventional road and rail links.

In the pipeline

Pipelines offer one of the cheapest and most efficient means of transporting liquid fuels, water, and chemicals over large distances. Today, many pipelines are monitored and maintained by computers. During the 21st century, advances in robotics will mean new pipelines can be laid with little or no human help. Using waterflow to carry solid materials, such as iron ore and coal, is likely to increase.

Support your railroads

Many governments encourage more use of public transportation and rail systems to ease overcrowded roads. We can expect to see increased investment in mass-transit systems, including driverless trains running underground or suspended from overhead tracks. High-speed trains, running at 280 mph. (450km/h) or more, may either be electric or powered by magnetic levitation. Analysts predict that they will carry as many as a third of all overland passengers by 2040.

CRYSTAL BALL

By 2050, pipelines pumped full of air under pressure may transport capsules containing goods above and below ground, as well as through water. These capsule systems may also carry people.

SEA TRANSPORTATION

▷ Until the arrival of steamships in the early 1800s, long-distance sea journeys had to be made on sailing ships. They relied on the wind, which was unpredictable, to move forward.

Sail revival

A new form of a traditional technology is likely to appear on many ships. By 2015, tankers and giant container ships may be fitted with sails to complement the regular engines. The sails will be computer-controlled to take advantage of the wind, regardless of what direction it is blowing. Although this system depends on weather conditions, it can reduce fuel consumption by as much as 25 percent.

It has been almost a century since sea transportation provided the fastest and, in some cases, the only link between distant places. However, shipping continues to be one of the most effective methods of moving goods and materials around the planet. New propulsion systems will help cut transportation times and this will encourage more industries to move freight by sea. Passenger vessels will also grow in popularity. On short journeys, small ferries can carry people across the water at high speed. At the other end of the scale is a new generation of ocean liners that can carry up to 5,000 people and feature a mall, ice skating rink, and even artificial beaches on board.

▷ This ground-effect craft of the year 2030 skims the surface on a cushion of air created by its giant wings. Ground-effect craft will also be able to cross flat, isolated areas and icy wastes.

Magnet power

Magnetohydrodynamic (MHD) propulsion could become a common form of sea propulsion by the 2030s. MHD uses a superconducting magnet to generate a powerful electric field around tubes filled with seawater. An electric current passes through the water and generates a strong force that drives the water out of the tubes and the craft forward. MHD has no moving parts, takes up little room, works well at high speeds and creates little noise or vibration. MHD propulsion may power new generations of superfast, short-distance ferries, as well as long-distance cruisers and military "stealth" ships.

△ The *Solar Sailor* uses large modules of waterproofed solar cells to provide power. The sails can be tilted at any angle to catch the sunlight as well as the wind.

◁ The *Yamato 1* is the world's first boat to be powered by magnetohydrodynamic propulsion. Thrust is provided by an electric current that passes through seawater. Future vessels will be capable of speeds up to 55 mph. (90km/h).

Flying boats

By 2020, a new kind of vessel that looks —and acts—more like a plane than a ship may be in operation. Ground-effect craft will use the extra lift generated by a wing flying a few feet above the surface of the water to cruise at speeds of up to 280 mph. (450km/h). The reduced drag created by this form of propulsion will make these craft extremely fuel efficient. Ground-effect craft will be able to carry very large payloads—or up to 600 passengers—but at a much lower cost than conventional air transportation.

△ Sailing boats are still a popular choice for recreational and sporting activities. Advanced sail systems and computer-controlled weather and navigation systems make these lightweight yachts safer and extremely maneuverable.

▷ The *Carnival Destiny*, built in 1996, can carry over 2,500 passengers in great luxury. It is as long as three football fields and, at 184 feet (56m), is taller than the Statue of Liberty.

IMPERIAL AIRWAYS
FOR SPEED AND COMFORT

◁ During the 1930s, air travel was a luxury that only the wealthy could afford. Aircraft seated small numbers of people and usually had to land and refuel nearly every 200 miles.

AIRPORTS AND AIR TRAVEL

The number of air passengers is expected to triple over the first twenty years of the 21st century, placing enormous demands on airports around the world. Many airports are already at their full capacity. Building more runways is not the answer because city locations and crowded airspace mean there is little room for further expansion. One solution is to build bigger airliners and new airports. Floating airports are another possibility, as is the use of land reclaimed from the sea. However, the most radical changes to airports are likely to take place inside the passenger terminals.

▷ In the future, faster processing of passengers, and more reliable aircraft will help prevent unnecessary delays, and overcrowded scenes such as this one at Gatwick Airport in England.

Smoother procedures

Automated passenger handling systems will remove many of the lengthy administration procedures that affect air travelers today. By 2010, advanced imaging systems and powerful computers will mean that procedures such as passport control and security checks can be performed automatically, without the delays caused by human intervention. Time spent on the ground will be significantly reduced and this in turn will help reduce overcrowding in terminals.

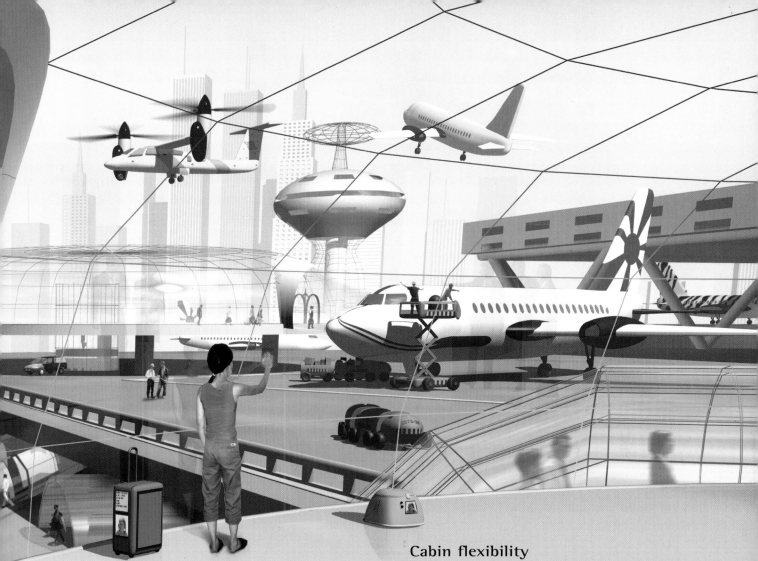

△ Electronic tagging will insure your baggage never gets lost. Screens built into the casing will display all relevant flight information.

◁ Electronic passport control, as well as body and baggage checks, will be performed by a single walk-through scanner system. This will allow faster departures and arrivals.

▽ Some airlines have already introduced automated ticket dispensers that reduce check-in, ticketing, and boarding times.

Local air transportation

Short flights from city to city or even within a metropolitan area are likely to receive a major boost by 2010 with the arrival of fleets of tilt-rotor aircraft. These aircraft are capable of short and vertical takeoffs and landings because they can tilt their turboshaft engines upward. For regular flight, the engines are returned to a horizontal position. With cruise speeds of around 300 mph. (500km/h), tilt-rotor aircraft are faster, quieter, and more fuel-efficient than helicopters.

Cabin flexibility

In the early years of the 21st century, air travelers can expect to see two new trends. For short flights, some aircraft will be designed without cargo holds, but with larger cabin storage instead. These fast-track flights will offer quick, regular services for walk-on, walk-off passengers. For long-distance flights, travelers who can afford it will have their own private sleeping cabins. These will be constructed with foldaway beds and ceiling storage to maximize space.

△ Hong Kong Airport opened in 1998. Its main terminal is nearly a mile long, has driverless trains, and 54 moving walkways. The airport can handle up to 87 million passengers a year.

AIRLINERS

Aircraft have come a long way since the first wood and canvas contraptions took to the air at the beginning of the 1900s. Air travel has transformed millions of people's lives by making it possible to travel abroad or make long journeys, which in the past would have taken days or even months. Aircraft will become faster and continue to grow in size, some carrying up to a thousand passengers at a time. Long-range aircraft that do not need to refuel will cut traveling time on longhaul flights by up to a third. But the most exciting proposals are for high-speed airliners that use rocket engines to blast the craft into space.

△ The de Havilland Comet was the world's first jet airliner. It began passenger service in 1952 and could carry 36 passengers.

Increased capacity

In 1997, there were over 1.6 billion air travelers. This figure is expected to rise to over 5 billion by 2020. To cope with the additional demand, larger aircraft will be built for the more popular routes. Two-tiered airliners carrying up to 700 passengers will be in service by 2020 and 900-seat models by 2030. Airports and boarding procedures will also have to be radically altered to cope with the rapid increase in passenger numbers.

△ The Airbus Industries A3XX is expected to be in service by 2006. This new type of mega-jumbo will seat 555 passengers and have a range of over 8,000 miles (14,000km) . Future versions will carry over 650 people.

The pursuit of speed

The first supersonic aircraft began flying regular passenger services in the 1970s. The Concorde can fly at speeds of 1,488 mph. (2,400 km/h)—almost three times the speed of conventional aircraft. The next generation of high-speed craft will be be hypersonic, flying at Mach 5 and above (Concorde cruises just above Mach 2). Some hypersonic designs will be suborbital—powerful rocket engines will boost the aircraft into partial orbit around the earth. The aircraft will then glide down to its destination.

▽▷ Hypersoar will use its engines to fly to the edge of the earth's atmosphere and into space. It will then shut down its engines and glide down to an altitude of 25 miles (40km) before firing its engines again. This trajectory prevents it overheating in the extremely hot atmosphere. Hypersoar will carry passengers to the other side of the world in under two hours.

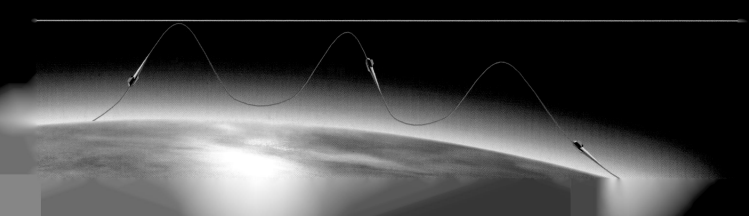

Out of this world

One of the most revolutionary proposals for future aircraft design is the Hypersoar craft. Hypersoar will skim the top of the earth's atmosphere in a unique skipping trajectory, operating its engines in short bursts. It will fly and coast back to earth at speeds of up to 6,200 mph. (10,000 km/h). By 2035, Hypersoar aircraft could be in operation flying express mail and special services. Larger, passenger-carrying craft may be launched five or ten years later.

BLURRED VISION

At the beginning of the 1900s some people envisaged that a constant traffic of flying machines would fill the skies. Here, flying taxis and private craft hover and fly above Paris.

▷ The X-34 reusable rocket is likely to be the successor to the space shuttle. Some of its technology is likely to be used in suborbital and hypersonic airliners.

1760s
Industrial Revolution in Great Britain changes the way people work

1800s
Development of organized rules for many sports

1870s
First practical typewriters used in offices

1938
Photocopy machines appear

1950
First credit cards in use

1960s
Cost of air travel plummets–air travel now available to many people

1980s
Arrival of affordable personal computers

WORK AND PLAY

In the last two decades of the 1900s, computers and new technology dramatically changed the the way we work and live. The Information Revolution will continue to transform society in almost every area, from education to recreational pursuits. Full-time jobs will become increasingly scarce with a growing number of people doing part-time work. Many offices will close as people work from home, linked by videophones, teleconferencing, and intelligent computer networks a thousand times faster than the current Internet. The search for work will involve scouring the whole globe, not just the local area. When not working, you will be able to visit local artificial resorts, climate-controlled by technology to mimic more distant and exotic locations. However, as everyday environments become increasingly secure and controlled, some people will seek thrills by pursuing new adrenaline-inducing sports.

2060
Machines directly
controlled by the mind

2040
First vacations in
orbiting space hotels

2010s
Huge increase in
telecommuting

THE WAY TO WORK

Today we are living in the early years of the Information Revolution. The number of people in manufacturing industries will continue to go down—by 2025, less than two percent of the workforce in the developed world will work in factories. Jobs that involve computers and communications will continue to increase. Other major growth areas will include tourism and professional care for an increasingly aging population. Many jobs were once for life. In the future, most employment will be short-term, away from a fixed base, and will rely on technology to link workers and customers.

△ In the early part of the 1900s, working conditions in offices were often cramped and uncomfortable.

△▷ By 2010, wearable computers will provide complete office facilities for workers on the move. An alternative to the office-on-the-arm system uses a headset to create the illusion of a full-size computer screen.

Telecommuting

Many people already work from home. In the future, telecommuting will continue to grow, affecting millions of workers, from technical support staff to salespeople. Links to customers and coworkers will be provided by high-speed data networks, multiline telephone systems, and real-time, high-quality video cameras. Computers could even be used to measure aspects of an employee's work performance.

◁ A laptop computer linked to a modem and satellite mobile phone allows people working in the most isolated areas to keep in touch with colleagues almost anywhere in the world.

▽ Many meetings in the workplace of the future are likely to use advanced communications, such as this 3-D holographic system, to bring people together. Holography uses lasers to produce lifelike images.

Flexible workers

Current work trends such as short-term contracts, more women in work, and more part-time jobs will continue well into the 21st century. It is estimated that by 2010, more than 40 percent of the workforce will be women. Despite the growth of teleworking, however, not everyone will operate from home—a significant part of the workforce will become much more mobile. Fewer international barriers and restrictions will allow more people to travel abroad in a global search for different kinds of work.

Future offices

Although more people will work at home, offices will not disappear. Many will evolve into communication centers for employees to use. The buildings will become spaces for workers on the move and the offices will be highly flexible. Staff will find themselves hotdesking—using whatever desk is available when they come into work. Smart desks with built-in global communications and computer and copying facilities will recognize and respond to each user.

◁ VR technology will be used increasingly in the design and testing of products before they are built. Here, engineers and technicians are studying the construction of a car.

△ Teleconferencing uses real-time cameras to provide instant visual communication with people in different places. By 2020, teleconferencing will become more realistic with a new generation of holographic systems.

△ In the early part of the 1900s, teaching in many schools relied on strict discipline and inflexible learning techiques.

In the Information Age, knowledge is power. The ability to access information, understand it, and communicate it to others has become highly prized. Education will play a central role in developing these skills. On-line teaching, virtual classrooms, and electronic books (ebooks) will be an essential part of education by the 2020s. Virtual teachers will be increasingly available to many preschool children. Traditional elements of school life such as group activities, field trips, and printed books will not disappear altogether, but they may be eclipsed by technological alternatives.

FUTURE LEARNING

The end of print?

The arrival of affordable ebooks may revolutionize how we read. Ebooks are electronic versions of books and magazines downloaded from the Internet that can be stored and read on a regular PC or on a special, lightweight, handheld reading device. The reading devices can hold thousands of book pages in their memory. Ebooks waste no paper, but still allow users to scribble notes on the text with electronic pens. By 2050, printed books may become collectors' items.

School days

By 2030, students might spend more time working from home. Structured classes will use 3-D holographic projection systems while high-speed data links will enable teachers and students to hold teleconferences. However, time spent interacting with other students at school will continue to be an important part of education.

△ Every generation can benefit from learning with computers. The ability to have interactive classes over the Internet may revolutionize education in the 21st century.

▷ Learning how to use a computer is becoming one of the basic skills for children in the early years of education.

◁ Books still offer unique advantages over computers. They are cheap, portable, and provide easy access to information. However, in the next few decades, books may be replaced by ebooks.

Continuous education

In the future, education will not end when you are 18 or 21. In the rapidly changing Information Age, learning will become a lifelong process. People will need to acquire many new skills during their lifetime. Adults may work on three or more degrees, while learning aids accessed by computers will provide introductions to new subjects and instant updating sessions for many skills.

▷ Interactive displays are fun and important ways of learning at many zoos, museums, and wildlife parks. At the London Aquarium, the public is encouraged to interact with some of the marine life.

△ Virtual reality headsets and data gloves may feature in many schools and homes by 2020. VR can help explain complex topics, such as the atomic structure of elements, in an exciting and effective way.

△ At the end of the 1800s, Egypt had become a destination for wealthy tourists. Mass tourism, however, only emerged with the arrival of cheap airfares in the 1960s.

In the time that it takes you to read this sentence, over 3,000 people will be on a flight to travel to another country—some for business, but most for pleasure. Travel and tourism are the world's biggest industries, generating almost 12 percent of the global income. By 2025, the number of tourists is expected to double and at least four million new jobs in the travel and tourism industry will be created each year. There will also be a greater range of vacation options. Traditional destinations will remain popular, but people will also be offered new travel opportunities, such as vacations underwater and in space.

TOURISM AND TRAVEL

▽ Scuba divers are just one of the sights you can expect to see from your bedroom window in this underwater hotel off the coast of Florida.

Travel trends

In the future there will be fewer travel agents. This sector will suffer because of the ease and convenience of buying flights and accommodations directly over the Internet. Another technological innovation is likely to be in-ear translation systems. By 2020, an earpiece and tiny microphone will be able to translate most foreign languages in real-time with 90 percent accuracy.

New locations

Despite environmental pressures, it is likely that hotels will be built in the Arctic and Antarctic by 2025. By the middle of the 21st century, space hotels orbiting the earth may be a popular, though expensive, destination. Long before then, we can expect to see a boom in underwater resorts in seas and oceans. All these new destinations will rely on technology to create a comfortable and safe environment for the tourists.

Late in the 21st century, tourists may be able to choose destinations that lie beyond the earth. Water, found frozen in rocks on the moon, may be used as a source for a moon hotel and base.

Access denied

Although tourism generates a large amount of wealth, it can also create a number of problems. Tourism can damage the environment and threaten culturally important sites. The potentially destructive effects caused by a greater number of tourists could lead to a rise in environmental protests and many historical sites may be closed to the public.

▷ Since the 1990s, there has been an increased demand for unconventional vacations. Antarctica and other protected wilderness areas are becoming established destinations for high-paying tourists.

◁ By 2010, underwater hotels will operate in popular vacation areas, such as the Caribbean, Hawaii, and the South Pacific. Tourist submersibles will ferry people to and from hotels, as well as taking them on seabed sightseeing trips.

LEISURE ACTIVITIES

△ Soccer fans in the 1890s were crammed together in the open. Sports stadiums in the 21st century will offer a range of comforts and features, like LCD screens fitted into seats.

Predictions of a world in which most people are freed from work and household drudgery, so that they can live a life of complete leisure are not likely to become a reality during the 21st century. Even so, the amount of leisure time available to many people will increase because of shorter working hours, less commuting, labor-saving household devices, and services such as Internet shopping. Many traditional activities, including sports, will continue. But we can also expect virtual reality (VR) simulators, sophisticated interactive television, and the creation of new, indoor artificial environments.

◁ This three-dimensional version of the Spiderman cartoon character thrills visitors at Universal Studios in Orlando. Future VR systems will offer a greater level of realism and interaction.

◁ Giant fans generate wind conditions of up to 25 knots in this wind-surfing arena in Paris, France. Future sport centers will produce even more lifelike conditions.

▽ Sarcos is a robot capable of recognizing and reacting to a human table tennis player's moves. Robotic opponents are likely to become a popular feature of future game centers.

Inside the Dome

Not all recreational time will be spent at home. You may be able to visit an exotic location just a short journey from where you live. During the 21st century, we can expect to see a rise in the popularity of recreational domes. Such structures already exist in Japan. They recreate a variety of environments, like tropical beaches or winter resorts. The weather outdoors is never a problem because the domes are completely self-contained, and maintain a constant climate.

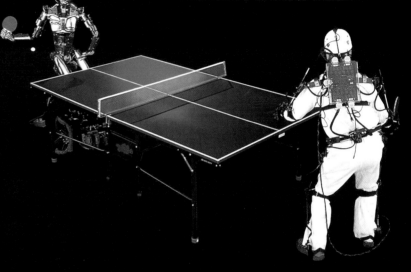

Stay at home

Future homes, equipped with the latest technology, may be the place where millions of people choose to spend their recreational time. Exercise machines that simulate outdoor activities will be a common feature as people spend more time indoors. Entertainment systems will become increasingly interactive. For example, you will probably be able to watch sporting events from a number of different camera angles or choose your own instant replays.

Another world

Virtual reality (VR), which generates a realistic three-dimensional world around a person, has the potential to revolutionize games and entertainment. By 2015, today's cumbersome VR helmets are likely to be replaced by lightweight displays or glasses that project images directly into the eye. By 2025, VR bodysuits will create a new level of realism by using a system of sensors and tiny mechanical devices that simulate all the senses.

▷ The Seagaia Ocean resort complex in Miyazaki, Japan, is the world's most advanced all-weather indoor resort. It can hold 10,000 visitors.

◁ Roller coasters have provided adrenaline-pumping excitement for millions of visitors to fairs and amusement parks since the first models were built in the late 1800s.

ADRENALINE SPORTS

For future generations, life in cities will become increasingly secure and structured. Many recreational activities will reflect this and use technology to create harmless artificial environments. For some people though, this will not be enough. There will be a major growth in activities that mimic the fear and the thrill people experience when they are in real danger. These activities are sometimes known as "adrenaline sports," after the chemical that the human body secretes when it is extremely excited. For those who want the thrills, but not the risks, microprocessor implants may be used to simulate these experiences by around 2050.

◁ A bungee jumper, attached only by a strong, elastic rope, free-falls through the air. The rope pulls jumpers back before they hit the ground.

Searching for the ultimate high

Traditional high-risk sports, such as free-fall parachuting, spelunking, and climbing, will continue to attract people looking for an element of danger in their recreational activities. Newer, extreme sports and activities will also evolve—including illegal ones such as hangliding from the tops of tall buildings.

▷ River rapids make white-water rafting a dangerous, though exciting, activity. Rafts are usually inflatable and made of tough nylon fabric. White-water rafting is likely to continue to grow in popularity.

Safe fighting

While organized sports provide an outlet for some people's violent feelings, a new breed of aggression-releasing activities will be developed during the 21st century. Impact-resistant headguards and bodysuits will allow people to fight and wrestle without the risk of physical injury. Virtual reality bodysuits will also be in use by 2020. They will enable people to battle each other or a computer-generated opponent from the safety of an arcade or their own homes.

◁ Sky-surfers surf the air on specially adapted snowboards before opening their parachutes and dropping to the ground. We can expect to see a growth in these kinds of hybrid sports as people seek new challenges.

▽ Street lugers ride on lightweight boards mounted on low-friction wheels that can reach speeds of up to 80 mph. (130km/h). A more extreme version—bodyblading—in which the wheels are attached directly to a bodysuit could provide a new activity for adrenaline seekers during the 21st century.

All in the mind

One day, microprocessor-controlled implants may simulate adrenaline highs even more realistically than third or fourth generation virtual reality systems. By 2040, surgical implants in the skull may use biofeedback to both record and shape thought patterns in the brain.

2050
Cloud seeding machines used to create rain

2020
Human body parts—grown in animals—are available

2010
Common medicines are grown in plants with biotechnology

2005
Human Genome Project completed

HEALTHY LIVING

During the 21st century, people will live longer and lead healthier lives than ever before. Improved health care, breakthroughs in the understanding of the human body, and even the possibility of developing "spare" body parts will improve the lives of millions of people. Advances in genetics will allow doctors to screen and treat people—even babies still in the womb—for many diseases that are currently incurable. Major developments are also expected in biotechnology and farming. Increases in food production, combined with more effective water management, have the potential to prevent the terrible famines and droughts that afflicted many developing nations during the 1900s. The cost of good health care, an increasingly aging population, and providing enough food and water worldwide will dominate the politics of many countries over the next century.

1978
First test-tube baby born in England

1958
Heart pacemaker invented

1955
First successful polio vaccine

1928
Discovery of penicillin

1851
Mechanical reaper revolutionizes farming

1796
First vaccinations developed by Edward Jenner

△ Freshwater was not readily available for most people before the 1900s. Today, in some countries, many people still do not have access to water in their homes.

In developed nations, clean water, waste disposal, and sanitation are often taken for granted—until there are water shortages or blockages in pipes and drains. For millions of people in developing nations, however, this is not the case. For them, sanitation and access to clean water can mean the difference between life and death. During the 21st century, new techniques in supplying and generating water, combined with improvements in weather forecasting, will have a global benefit.

WEATHER, WATER, AND WASTE

△ Global warming may become partly responsible for major droughts during the 21st century. These will put a great strain on the world's water supplies.

The big issues

Although freshwater is abundant on a global scale, it is often scarce locally. It has been estimated that over a billion people around the world lack access to safe water. More effective and fairer distribution of water will become a priority during the 21st century. Governments should insure that existing water supplies, such as rivers, do not become contaminated as a result of pollution.

Disposal

Over 7 gallons (30l) of freshwater are used each time a toilet is flushed. Waste needs to be removed, but alternatives that use as little water as possible in the process need to be found. Waterless toilets, which use layers of bacteria in sealed tanks to digest waste and turn it into harmless compost, are one possibility. They require no water and prevent the spread of disease.

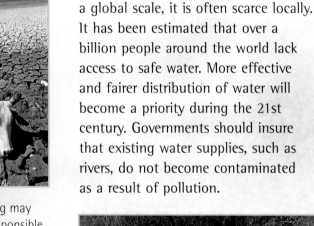

◁ Huge quantities of industrial waste, called effluent, are poured into rivers, polluting water supplies. If this continues, many valuable sources of freshwater will become unsuitable for human consumption, even after treatment at water purification plants..

◁ Desalination plants use up large amounts of energy, but are capable of turning saltwater into freshwater. Future plants may be considerably more energy efficient.

Freshwater for all

In areas where water is scarce, efforts may turn to water generation rather than collection and distribution. Cost-effective extraction of freshwater from saltwater at desalination plants may be likely in the near future. By 2050, altering the chemical structure of clouds, or cloud seeding, may be used to make rain where it is needed most.

△ The Meteosat weather satellite, built by the European Space Agency, transmits an image of cloud patterns back to a ground base on Earth every 30 minutes.

◁ By the middle of the 21st century, vast fleets of insect-sized cloud seeding machines, or mesicopters, may be launched in areas with little rainfall. Once inside the clouds, the mesicopters will release chemical particles that cause water vapor to form and fall as rain.

▷ The development of new materials and advances in microengineering will allow the manufacture of cheap and extremely small machines.

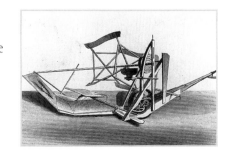

▷ The mechanical reaping machine, invented by Cyrus Hall McCormick in 1851, allowed farmers to quadruple the amount of grain they could harvest.

FUTURE FARMING

For thousands of years, most of the world's population farmed the land. Crops were grown and animals were raised to support each family. Any surplus was taken to the market to be sold. During the 1700s, the Agricultural Revolution in Europe began a process that continues today—a small proportion of people produce food for the majority. During the 21st century, technology including "smart" harvesting machinery, biotechnology, and hydroponics will make farming more efficient. Even so, it will take a great deal of political action, as well as scientific advances, to end global hunger.

△ These Atlantic salmon are being farmed in Norway—10 percent of seafood is farmed in this way. This figure is likely to triple by 2025.

▷ It is likely that droughts and famines will continue long into the 21st century. Millions of people, like these refugees in Zaire, will rely on food aid from other countries to survive.

▷ Tea leaf pickers on an Indonesian plantation are likely to remain in work for decades to come. It will be a long time before robots and machines will be capable of harvesting such delicate crops.

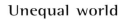

Unequal world

One of the great inequalities of the modern world is that, while some countries produce an amount of food surplus to their needs, millions still go hungry and die from starvation or malnutrition each year. This is likely to continue unless governments around the world take the initiative and there is a shift in attitudes. It is also hoped that food production levels can be raised by biotechnology, advances in pest control, and the creation of crops that can survive droughts and other weather extremes.

◁ In this greenhouse, a computer controlled watering unit provides the exact amount of water required for maximum plant growth.

Popular science has predicted that a person's nutritional needs will be found in a single pill. Although it may be possible, the benefits and enjoyment of eating a variety of foods means that it is unlikely to replace our current diet.

▷ Killing pests, such as slugs, can involve using dangerous chemical pesticides that dissolve into the soil. This pest control robot can collect and eradicate pests without using chemicals. Once caught, the slugs are turned into a biogas, which then powers the robot.

Farming fish

Fish and other sea products are a major source of protein. By 2015, worldwide demand for all forms of seafood is expected to increase by 50 percent. To meet this demand, the fishing industry will need to exploit new fishing grounds and invest more in aquaculture, or fish farming. Aquaculture takes place in lakes, ponds, and reservoirs, where the environment can be carefully controlled.

Robo-farmers

Farming is time-consuming, labor-intensive work. In developed nations, farming is a mechanized process. Many machines are used, from combine harvesters, to crop sorters, and packaging devices in factories. Future technology will be developed to increase production and reduce costs. By 2025, robots will probably tend delicate greenhouse plants, such as tomatoes, as well as harvest fruit crops. More automation will also be used in the rearing of livestock.

▷ Hydroponics may become an important branch of farming. Hydroponics is the growing of plants without using soil. This researcher is studying lettuce and tomato plants in a laboratory in Arizona.

◁▷ Biotechnology has the power to create uniquely patterned flowers, as well as the potential for more important uses, like longer lasting fruit and vegetables, or the creation of new medicines derived from plants, or even animals.

BIOTECHNOLOGY

Biotechnology is the name given to techniques used to control living organisms for the benefit of humans. Although it is linked in many people's minds with the genetic engineering of plants and animals in order to create new, hybrid species, this is only one part of the biotechnology story. Biotechnology has the potential to eradicate food shortages, to cure many diseases, and to produce eco-friendly fuels and materials. However, the debate about whether we should be tampering with nature will continue for some time.

Food supplies

People have been selecting seeds, growing plant hybrids, and interbreeding animals for centuries to produce more robust crops and livestock. Biotechnology could increase the amounts of crops worldwide. Damage inflicted by pests and diseases, as well as spoiling at farms, packaging factories, and stores means that as much as half of all fruit and vegetables grown never becomes available to the consumer. By creating longer lasting, disease resistant products, food production could receive an enormous boost by 2015.

△ A great part of biotechnology work on plants takes place in laboratories where genetically engineered seedlings can be grown and studied in controlled conditions.

Growing plastics

Plants are likely to provide a major source of materials in the future. In the 1920s, starch collected from plants began to be used to produce acetone and other paint solvents. In the future a new form of plastic may be grown and stored within genetically modified plants such as potatoes. Unlike today's plastic, which is manufactured using expensive and limited oil reserves, this plastic would be cheap to produce and would also be biodegradable.

Medical breakthroughs

Biotechnology has the potential to make radical changes in the way we obtain many important medicines. Turnips, for example, have already been modified to produce anticancer drugs. Another strand of biotechnology called "pharming" uses modified farm animals to generate important substances for the pharmaceutical industry. By 2025, "pharmed" livestock may provide our most important medicines.

△ Advances in biotechnology have resulted in the first self-shearing sheep. The sheep is injected with a special solution called Bioclip that contains a protein that causes wool fibers to break away.

▷ A researcher analyzes how a sweet sorghum plant reacts to different watering conditions. Sweet sorghum is a common cereal crop that scientists are studying to determine whether it can become a leading source of biofuel in the 21st century.

GENETIC ENGINEERING

Genes are the instructions that determine an organism's characteristics. In humans, for example, everything from hair and eye color to susceptibility to certain diseases is passed down, or inherited, from parents via genes. Genes are contained in a chemical called DNA, which is found in the cells of all living things. Identifying and understanding how to manipulate genes is revolutionizing science. Genetic illnesses may one day become a thing of the past. Unborn children may be tested for genetic defects and treated in the womb using a technique called gene therapy. However, the ability to fundamentally alter genes means that there are major concerns about the consequences of genetic engineering.

△ The British scientist Francis Crick and American James Watson discovered the double helix, or spiral, structure of DNA (deoxyribonucleic acid) in 1953.

Cloning

Scientists have been successful in creating identical copies, or clones, of existing plants and animals. In 1997, Dolly the sheep became the first mammal cloned from the cell of another adult mammal. However, cloning has been regarded with some suspicion—the ethics of creating identical humans has been a concern to many, but it is more likely to be used in medical research or to produce higher-yield crops.

◁ These baby mice glow green under a blue light. They have been genetically engineered to include a jellfyfish gene that causes them to become fluorescent. The gene may be used to mark and study cancerous cells in humans.

◁ Dolly is a genetic duplicate, or clone. She was created from a cell extracted from an adult sheep.

▷ The Human Genome Project (HGP) is providing a new understanding of our genetic make-up. Four chemicals, known as A, G, C and T, are found in each gene. Determining their order is a major part of the HGP.

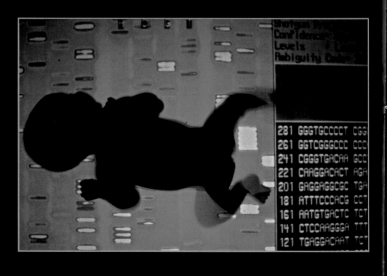

281 GGGTGCCCCT CGG
261 GGTCGGGCCC CCC
241 CGGGTGACAA GCC
221 CAAGGACACT AGA
201 GAGGAGGCGC TGA
181 ATTTCCCACG CCT
161 AATGTGACTC TCT
141 CTCCAAGGGA TTT
121 TGAGGACAAT TCT

▷ The corkscrew-shaped DNA chemical is present in every single cell. DNA stores genes, which are the instructions that determine an organism's traits. Although it can only be seen under an electron microscope, human DNA would stretch over 16 feet (5m) if it was unfolded.

△ Thousands of scientists are working across the world to determine the sequence of the coded information contained in human DNA.

▷ Special growth cells created by genetic engineering will play a major role in growing artificial skin and blood vessels.

Gene therapy

Genetic defects are responsible for almost 5,000 diseases. Gene therapy is a new form of treatment that involves the insertion of a healthy gene into a virus that has been neutralized so that it can do no harm. The modified virus, carrying the corrected gene, is then injected into the patient. In this way, inherited diseases, including haemophilia and cystic fibrosis—the most common genetic disorder in the Western world, may be successfully combated.

CRYSTAL BALL

The power to manipulate the genes of unborn children raises the fear of "designer" babies. In the future, unless prevented by law, parents will be able to specify the sex, looks, and even the behavior of their children.

Breaking the code

Begun in 1990, the Human Genome Project is one of the most ambitious and important scientific projects ever undertaken. Its main goal is to identify and map the 100,000 genes in human DNA. The Human Genome Project is expected to be completed before 2005. It will provide scientists with a revolutionary new tool for diagnosing, treating and, one day, potentially preventing most human diseases and disorders.

◁ Many doctors once believed that protective clothing would prevent them from catching their patients' illnesses. In the 1600s, doctors became known as "quacks." This came from the Dutch word "quacksalver," a seller of remedies.

Historically, the world's biggest killers have not been wars or natural disasters, but diseases. In 1918, for example, a new strain of influenza virus killed at least 40 million people. During the 1900s, the average life expectancy across the globe increased as we learned more about diseases and how to combat them. Even so, in the first half of the 21st century medical research will face some major challenges. These will include an increase of certain diseases as populations age, and the possibility of new viruses and superbugs that are immune to conventional treatments.

FINDING A CURE

◁ A woman from northern India is injected with a vaccine against tetanus. Vaccinating people has been one of the greatest victories in the fight against disease.

△ The smart pill, unlike other oral medicines, will target a specific area of the body. After the pill has been swallowed, its path through the digestive system will be traced by radio signals. Once the pill has reached its destination (in this case a growth in the large intestine) a signal will be sent to release the drugs.

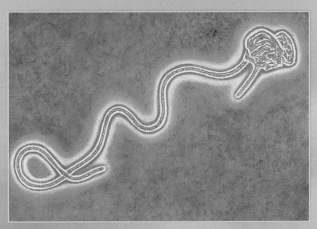

◁ The deadly Ebola virus, shown here at 19,000X magnification, is responsible for fever and, frequently, rapid death. Scientists must find new ways of treating such diseases. In many cases the overuse of antibiotics has created viruses that are drug-resistant.

Making the medicine go down

In the future, doctors will be able to tailor specific medicine treatments for each patient with much greater effectiveness. Genetic testing will help determine exact dosages and reduce side effects. Some medicine will be sprayed onto edible strips of paper, while others will be dispensed in smart pills. Controlled by microelectronics, smart pills will target a specific area of the body before releasing their cargo of medicine.

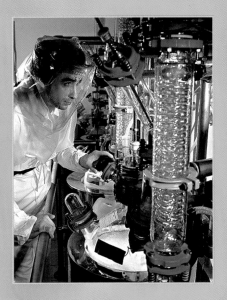

▷ Finding effective ways of dispensing medicines is an important aspect of medical research. This technician is testing a medicine that can be delivered by a simple spray system.

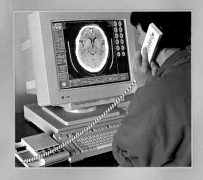

◁ A radiologist studies a patient's brain scan, which has been sent through a telephone line. Telemedicine may be used increasingly to allow specialists to make a diagnosis from almost anywhere in the world.

Screening

Preventive medicine and early diagnosis are the keys to reducing the number of premature deaths. Today's PET and MRI scanners will be joined by even more powerful screening tools that can peer into the body and detect potential problems and diseases much earlier. These include laser probes that can identify precancerous cells with extreme accuracy, and holographic medical imaging that will provide a three-dimensional view inside the body.

Prevention

As life expectancy increases, so does the likelihood of developing certain diseases including many cancers, heart disease, and diabetes. Our genetic make-up plays a major, but not exclusive, role in determining whether or not we become sick. During the 21st century there will be a greater emphasis on maintaining a healthy lifestyle in order to prevent disease. Diet, exercise, and low stress levels will be promoted as the most important factors for a long and healthy life.

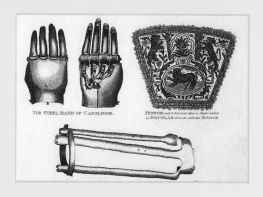

▷ During the 1800s, artificial limbs were very cumbersome and offered little flexibility. This 1815 engraving shows a steel hand and the metal frame that held it in place.

REPAIRING OUR BODIES

△ It takes only three weeks to grow just over one square yard of artificial skin from a tiny fragment. Artificial skin is used mainly to help burn victims.

Until the second half of the 20th century, when people lost a limb the most they could hope for was a crude, clumsy replacement. If a major internal organ such as the heart failed, recovery was rare. Since the 1960s, there have been advances in surgery, tissue engineering, artifical parts technology, and transplant operations. These developments have saved millions of lives and improved the quality of life for countless others. Further breakthroughs will mean that by 2025, most of your body—both inside and out—can be repaired, or damaged parts replaced.

▷ Human cartilage cells have been grafted onto the back of a hairless mouse in an attempt to grow a replica of a human ear.

Robotic assistance

Robots are capable of much greater precision and accuracy than human hands and will play an increasingly important role in surgery. The majority of robots will work as surgical assistants, controlled by surgeons. By 2020, computer networks will allow surgeons to operate remotely by controlling robots and other telesurgery machines, from a distance.

Tissue engineering

Currently, the demand for human body parts, especially internal organs, is higher than the supply. This will change, however, with advances in tissue engineering. This area of medical technology works to create tissues—and even new body parts—from human cells. Scientists have been successful growing skin, pieces of bone, and cartilage from human cells. Internal organs may be available by 2030. Known as neo-organs, these will be grown in laboratory conditions or even in animals acting as living hosts.

▷ MRI devices are powerful body imaging systems that have been beneficial to surgery and body repair. MRI stands for Magnetic Resonance Imaging and the devices produce detailed images of cross sections of the human body.

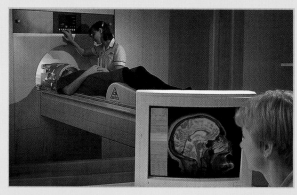

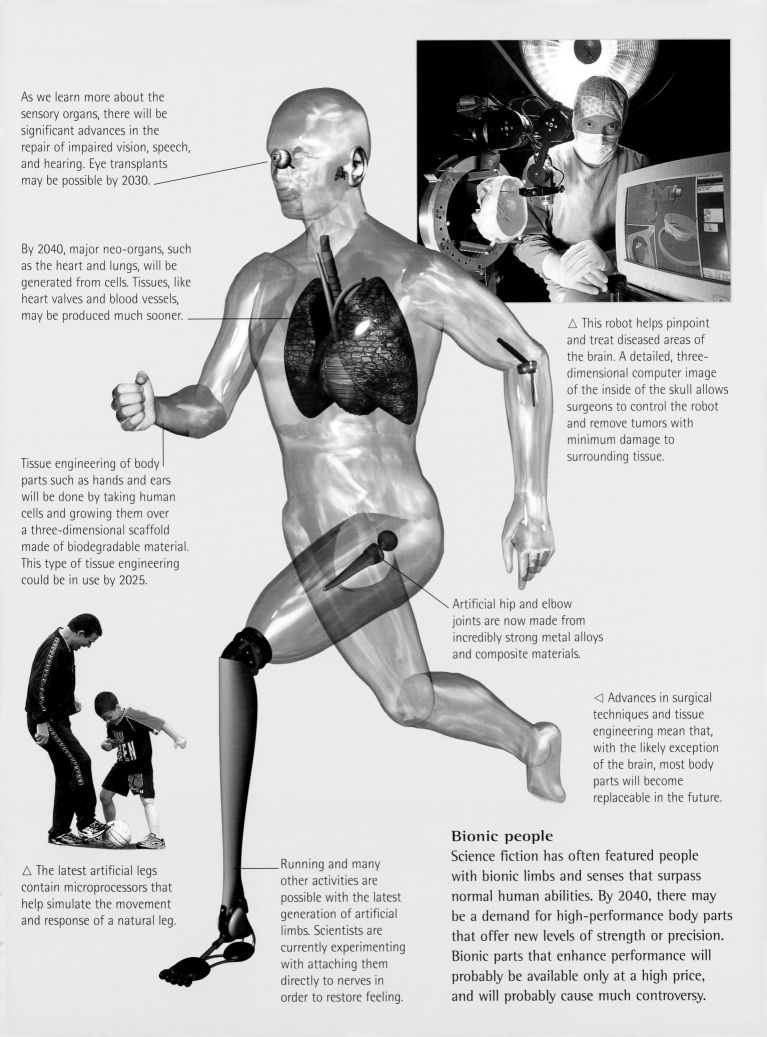

As we learn more about the sensory organs, there will be significant advances in the repair of impaired vision, speech, and hearing. Eye transplants may be possible by 2030.

By 2040, major neo-organs, such as the heart and lungs, will be generated from cells. Tissues, like heart valves and blood vessels, may be produced much sooner.

Tissue engineering of body parts such as hands and ears will be done by taking human cells and growing them over a three-dimensional scaffold made of biodegradable material. This type of tissue engineering could be in use by 2025.

△ This robot helps pinpoint and treat diseased areas of the brain. A detailed, three-dimensional computer image of the inside of the skull allows surgeons to control the robot and remove tumors with minimum damage to surrounding tissue.

Artificial hip and elbow joints are now made from incredibly strong metal alloys and composite materials.

◁ Advances in surgical techniques and tissue engineering mean that, with the likely exception of the brain, most body parts will become replaceable in the future.

△ The latest artificial legs contain microprocessors that help simulate the movement and response of a natural leg.

Running and many other activities are possible with the latest generation of artificial limbs. Scientists are currently experimenting with attaching them directly to nerves in order to restore feeling.

Bionic people

Science fiction has often featured people with bionic limbs and senses that surpass normal human abilities. By 2040, there may be a demand for high-performance body parts that offer new levels of strength or precision. Bionic parts that enhance performance will probably be available only at a high price, and will probably cause much controversy.

◁ Until the 1900s, people across the world frequently died in childhood. In this painting from the 1880s, a mother tends to her sick daughter.

In the early 1900s, the average person in the United States and Europe was not expected to live beyond 45 years. A person born in a developed country at the beginning of the 21st century can hope to live for twice as long. Advances in medicine and improvements in diet and lifestyle have been—and will continue to be—the key to longer life expectancy. Research into our genetic make-up may even one day enable us to slow down the aging process. For the forseeable future, however, it is likely that the gap between the life exectancies of the developing and developed nations will remain.

HOLDING
BACK the YEARS

Rise of the old

An increasing, aging population will have a profound effect on society. It is predicted that the number of retired people will double by 2020 and that caring for the elderly will become one of the biggest industries. Because people will remain active for longer, society will find new ways to use their skills. Political parties may be formed to represent this growing and powerful section of the population.

The aging process

Some scientists believe that there is a maximum age that human beings can reach. Others think that there is no natural limit and that locating the genes responsible for aging in humans is the key to a much longer life. Scientists have successfully used genetic engineering to increase the length of life of simple organisms such as worms and fruit flies. But it is still too early to tell if this will work in the more complex human body.

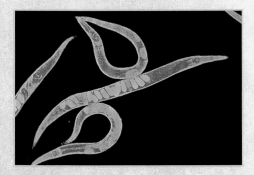

△ Nematode worms have been the focus of extensive research into genetic engineering. It has been shown that modified worms without a particular gene age more slowly than those with the gene.

◁ In parts of Mongolia there is an unusually high proportion of people who are over 100 years old. Careful study of such people can help scientists to discover the connections between long life and lifestyle and, maybe one day, specific genes that control aging.

Coming back from the dead

One possible way of defeating death is cryonics. This involves deep-freezing a person's body soon after death in the hope that advances in medical technology will allow that individual to be revived in the future. Either the whole body or just the head is immersed in liquid nitrogen at -320°F (-196°C) before the body tissue has had a chance to decay. One of the challenges of this technology will be to restore a fully functioning brain with all its memories still intact.

▷ A number of people with fatal or terminal diseases have paid to be kept frozen in low-temperature capsules after they die. It is hoped that, sometime in the future, doctors will be able to revive and cure them.

▽ During the 21st century, as life expectancy increases, the number of retired people will continue to rise.

GLOSSARY

Biotechnology The use of living organisms in industry, agriculture, and science.

Cloning The process of creating copies of living things from a single cell without sexual reproduction taking place. The new copy, or clone, is physically and genetically identical to the parent cell.

Cloud seeding The application of chemicals to clouds in order to control rain.

Cryonics Preserving a dead person's body at -310F°, in the hope of being able to revive it in the future.

Desalination The removal of salt and other minerals from seawater to create freshwater.

DNA A complex molecule, with a double-helix shape, that contains the genetic code for a living organism.

Gene therapy The identification and replacement of genes responsible for certain diseases with healthy genes.

Genetic engineering The transfer of genes between species to create new organisms that do not occur naturally in nature.

Genome The sum total of DNA within a species.

Ground-effect craft Vehicles, often seacraft, that have wings to create extra lift. They skim at high speed across flat surfaces.

Hypersonic Term used for speeds above five times the speed of sound. At sea level the speed of sound is 7,599 mph. (1,225 km/h).

Information Revolution The changes in the ways people work and how information is managed, brought on by improvements in computers and telecommunications.

Invasive surgery An operation that involves a large incision or cut being made in the patient for the doctor to perform surgery.

Laser A highly-focused beam of light or other radiation used to cut through objects or to carry information through optical fibers.

Magnetic Levitation A method of lifting objects by using magnetic attraction or the forces that keep magnets apart. Using a series of powerful magnets, it is possible for magnetic levitation to propel passenger-carrying trains at speeds of over 279 mph. (450 km/h).

Magnetohydrodynamic (MHD) A new method of propulsion for seacraft. It uses superconducting magnets to generate a powerful electric field around thruster tubes filled with seawater.

Mass transit systems Transportation systems, such as subways, traveling walkways, and bus networks designed to move large numbers of people.

Non-invasive surgery Surgery that relies on medical instruments inserted through a small incision in the patient's body.

Pharming The manufacture of medical products, particularly pharmaceutical products from genetically modified plants or animals. Still in its infancy, this technology could lead to cheap medicines as well as products

such as milk or plants that contain vaccines against human diseases.

Streamlining The design and shape of machines, particularly vehicles such as cars, boats and aircraft, so that they travel through the water or air more smoothly and efficiently.

Telesurgery The ability to send important medical information over a computer network so that a diagnosis can be made even though patient and doctor are in different places.

Teleworking Working from home and using technology such as computers, the Internet, and fax machines to stay in touch with a central office and clients.

Tissue engineering The artificial creation of parts of the body using a variety of techniques.

Transgenic organism Any living organism that has had its genetic make-up manipulated and altered so that it includes one or more genes from a different species.

Virtual reality A system that uses computers and senors to generate an artificial environment with which a human user can interact in a realistic way.

Virus A tiny organism that lives inside the cells of animals, plants, and bacteria. Viruses can only reproduce inside cells and frequently cause diseases. In computing, a virus is a self-replicating computer program that often creates havoc by damaging other programs and erasing data in memory.

WEBSITES

There are thousands of websites that relate to technology in our lives. Here are a few of them:

The Philips' *Vision of the Future* site at www.design.philips.com/vof/toc1/home.htm is full of exciting ideas for future technology that will affect our lives in many ways.

The exciting prospect of large numbers of ground-effect vehicles is considered in detail at the following site: www.io.tudelft.nl/~twaio/edwin/html/index.htm

Scientific American is a well-respected journal that reveals important scientific breakthroughs and makes future predictions. To explore the future of transportation, medicine, weather prediction, and food production, visit the magazine's website at: www.sciam.com/

The magazine *Popular Science* examines the latest developments in technology and its impact. Its website can be found at: **www.popsci.com**

You can find out about advances in land, sea, and air transportation at: **www.pbs.org/wgbh/nova/barrier**

If you are interested in learning more about travel and transportation, both in the present and the future, consider a visit to the biggest list of travel and transportation related links and resources on the Internet: **www.obd.nl/~otto/liste.htm**

The one-stop center if you want to learn more about the Human Genome Project is located at: **www.ornl.gov/TechResources/Human_Genome/home.html**

For information about robotics, try the NASA site at **www.robotics.jpl.nasa.gov**, which also includes links to other robot-related sites.

Other sites devoted to the history of medicine, transportation, agriculture, and other related topics can be reached using your favorite search engine.

PLACES OF INTEREST

Many museums and science centers around the country have displays and exhibitions that explore everyday life in the future. Some of them also feature the latest and forthcoming developments. They include:

The National Museum of American History (Washington, DC) An exhibition entitled *Information Age: People, Information, and Technology* shows, visually and interactively, how information technology has changed our society over the last 150 years.

The Tech Museum of Innovation (San Jose, CA) Over 240 interactive, hands-on exhibits about the technologies that affect our daily lives. The *Communication Gallery* explores the ways in which technology is making this a smaller world by changing how we work, communicate, and share information.

The National Air and Space Museum (Washington, DC) Many galleries are devoted to both the history of space flight and exploration. The museum features displays about future developments.

The Lawrence Hall of Science (Berkeley, CA) Explore a life size replica of the space shuttle, experiment with everyday uses of lasers, and interact with real robots to discover what the future may bring.

Museum of Science & Space Transit Planetarium (Jacksonville, FL) To gain an understanding of some of the changes that may affect everyday life in the future, test the echo tube, which lets you hear the speed of sound and listen as it travels through the air, direct a laser beam to make it refract, bounce, and focus, and view yourself in the anti-gravity mirror that makes you appear to fly. Also explore the momentum machine exhibit.

INDEX

ACKNOWLEDGMENTS

The publishers would like to thank the following illustrators
for their contribution to this book:

Julian Baum 10–11, 12–13, 30–31, 38–39, 54–55; Nik Clifford 3, 14–15,
28–29, 34–35, 36–37, 46–47, 49, 57; Graham Humphries 12, 25, 39, 53;
Dean McCallum 26–27; Mark Preston 6–7, 8–9, 18–19, 32–33, 44–45,
50–51, 58–59; Real–Time Visualisation 16–17, 22–23.

The publishers would like to thank the following for supplying photographs:

Front cover bc SuperStock Ltd; 8 c Hulton Getty, cr Arcaid/Richard Bryant, bl Hulton Getty; 10 tl Mary Evans Picture Library, cl Science Photo Library/David Parker, bl Science Photo Library/M-Sat Ltd; 11 tc Science Photo Library/David Nunuk; 12 tl Mary Evans Picture Library, bc Still Pictures/Shehzad Nooran; 13 t Frank Spooner Pictures/Gamma, cr Arcaid/Ian Lambot, bc Mary Evans Picture Library; 14 tl Hulton Getty, bl Science Photo Library/George Olson; 15 TR Environmental Images/Martin Bond, br Frank Spooner Pictures/Gamma; 17 tl Science & Society Picture Library/Louis Hine/NMPFT, Bradford, cl Science Photo Library/David Parker, cr Science Photo Library/John Mead, br Frank Spooner Pictures/Auenturier; 18 l Mary Evans Picture Library, c Mary Evans Picture Library, cr Science & Society Picture Library/Science Museum, r Rex Features; 19 l Rex Features, cl Rex Features, cr Quadrant Picture Library; 20 tl Hulton Getty, br Rex Features/Peter Brooker; 20-21 c Rex Features; 21 tr Ford Motor Company, cr Quadrant Picture Library, br Vin Mag Archive Ltd; 22 t Hulton Getty, c Mercedes-Benz; 23 tl Rex Features, tr Rex Features, c Rex Features/Nils Jorgensen, b Frank Spooner Pictures/Gamma Liaison; 24 tl Mary Evans Picture Library, bl Robert Harding Picture Library/HP Merten, br Still Pictures/Hartmut Schwarzbach; 24-25 t Quadrant Picture Library; 26 t The Bridgeman Art Library/British Library; 27 t Solar Sailor, tl Rex Features, cl Tony Stone Images/Alastair Black, bc Rex Features, br Colorific/Paul Van Riel/Black Star; 28 tr Vin Mag Archive Ltd, bc Rex Features; 29 c British Airways, br Dennis Gilbert; 30 tl TRH, c Frank Spooner Pictures; 31 l Science Photo Library/Marshall Space Flight Center/NASA, r Martin Breeze/Retrograph Archive Ltd; 32 cl Science & Society Picture Library/Daily Herald Archive/NMPFT, c Rex Features, cr Rex Features, r Science & Society Picture Library/Science Museum; 34 tl Mary Evans Picture Library, bl Rex Features/Simon Hadley, bc Science Photo Library/Sam Ogden; 35 tl Tony Stone Images/Wayne R. Bilenduke, bl Science Photo Library/James King-Holmes, br Rex Features; 36 tl Mary Evans Picture Library, cr Tony Stone Images/Walter Hodges, bl John Walmsley, BR Science Photo Library/Blair Seitz; 37 tr Camera Press/Stewart Mark; 38 tl Mary Evans Picture Library, cl Telegraph Colour Library/Jose Azel/Aurora; 39 TR Robert Harding Picture Library/Bill O'Connor, c Robert Harding Picture Library/Geoff Renner, br Planet Earth Pictures/Gary Bell; 40 tl Mary Evans Picture Library, bl Frank Spooner Pictures/Gamma presse images; 41 tl Allsport/Sylvain Cazenave, cr Katz Pictures/George Steinmetz/National Geographic Society; bc Rex Features; br Rex Features; 42 tl Mary Evans Picture Library/Barry Norman Collection, bl Allsport/Anne-Marie Weber; 42-43 c Rex Features, 43 tr Allsport/Didier Givois, br Allsport/Simon Bruty; 44 cr Science Photo Library/Laguna Design; 45 l Rex Features, cl Science & Society Picture Library/Science Museum, c Mary Evans Picture Library, br Science & Society Picture Library/Science Museum; 46 tl Mary Evans Picture Library, cl Rex Features/Pierre Schwartz/Sipa Press, bl Science Photo Library/Novosti Press Agency, br Science Photo Library/Simon Fraser; 47 tr Science Photo Library/David Ducros; 48 tr Hulton Getty, cl Still Pictures/Michel Roggo, cr Robert Harding Picture Library, b Still Pictures/Mark Edwards; 49 tl Still Pictures/Peter Frischmuth, tr Mary Evans Picture Library, b Science Photo Library/Peter Menzel; 50 c Science Photo Library/Tek Image; 51 tr Commonwealth Scientific and Industrial Research Organisation, c Science Photo Library/Tommaso Guicciardini; 52 tl Science Photo Library/A.Barrington Brown, c Science Photo Library/Makoto Iwafuji/Eurelios, bl Rex Features/Jeremy Sutton Hibbert, br Science Photo Library/Peter Menzel; 53 tl Still Pictures/Robert Holmgren, tr Science Photo Library/Laguna Design, c Science Photo Library/Peter Yates; 54 tl Mary Evans Picture Library, bl Science Photo Library/Simon Fraser; 55 tl Science Photo Library/Barry Dowsett, cl Science Photo Library/Simon Fraser, cr Science Photo Library/Geoff Tompkinson; 56 tr Mary Evans Picture Library/Webber, 1815, cl Science Photo Library/J.C. Revy, c BBC Photographic Library/Tomorrow's World, br Science Photo Library/ Geoff Tompkinson; 57 tr Science Photo Library/Klaus Guldbrandsen, bl Rex Features; 58 tl Mary Evans Picture Library; 59 tl Science Photo Library/James King-Holmes, tr Still Pictures/Adrian Arbib, ctr Frank Spooner Pictures/Gamma Liaison.

Key: b = bottom, c = center, l=left, t = top, r = right

Every effort has been made to trace the copyright holders of the photographs. The publishers apologize for any inconvenience caused.

The publishers would like to thank the following: Kate Amy, Preston Carter, Sinead Derbyshire, Cormac Jordan, Malcolm Lee, Gerhardt Meurer of Johns Hopkins University, William Murray and Danny Wooton.